TO ALL THE CURIOUS KIDS: Keep interrupting, asking, and thinking out loud. Be your own advocate and learn your way through life! Stay honest. Stay bold.

TO THE PARENTS: Take these quotes seriously enough to address, and lightly enough to laugh.

TO THE TEACHERS: We have a very important job—keep igniting curiosity!

I DID MY HOMEWORK IN MY HEAD

(AND OTHER WACKY THINGS KIDS SAY)

ALYSSA COWIT AND GREG DUNBAR

CLARKSON POTTER/PUBLISHERS
NEW YORK

Published in the United States by Clarkson
Potter/Publishers, an imprint of the Crown
Publishing Group, a division of
Penguin Random House LLC, New York.
crownpublishing.com
clarksonpotter.com

Clarkson Potter is a trademark and Potter
with colophon is a registered trademark of
Penguin Random House LLC.

Library of Congress
Cataloging-in-Publication Data
Names: Cowit, Alyssa, author. |
Dunbar, Greg, author.
Title: I did my homework in my head,
and other wacky things kids say /
Alyssa Cowit and Greg Dunbar.
Description: First edition. | New York : Potter
Style, 2017.
Identifiers: LCCN 2016020619| ISBN
9780451497031 (hardback) | ISBN
9780451497048 (ebook)
Subjects: LCSH: Children--Quotations. | BISAC:
HUMOR / Form / Anecdotes.
Classification: LCC PN6328.C5 C69 2017 | DDC
818/.602--dc23 LC record available at
https://lccn.loc.gov/2016020619

ISBN 978-0-451-49703-1
Ebook ISBN 978-0-451-49704-8

Printed in China
Book and cover design by Lise Sukhu
Illustrations by Lise Sukhu
10 9 8 7 6 5 4 3 2 1
First Edition

CONTENTS

Introduction

Acknowledgments

INTRODUCTION

After a long day of prepping, planning, and preaching, I asked my class, "What will you take home from the math lesson today?" A child sitting in the back of the class sheepishly raised his hand. "My butt has a line of symmetry!" All twenty-three of us had a good laugh. He couldn't have been more right!

Learning does not need to be serious; it can be outlandish, honest, and pure. What you'll find in these pages is a compilation of truthfulness, with good laughs mixed in—a hilarious look at what happens within the walls of elementary schools around the world.

What started as @LiveFromSnackTime on Instagram has now become a handpicked collection of outrageous classroom quotes. This book is proof that when kids are away from their families and surrounded by their peers, their curiosity and emotions are amplified. If you're an educator, we hope you'll laugh as you recall hearing similar things day in and day out. If you're a parent, you'll get insight as to what "School was good" actually means. Or maybe you'll simply reminisce about your own childhood discoveries.

—ALYSSA COWIT

EXCUSES

HOW TO GET WHAT YOU WANT

IF I DON'T WANT TO GO SOMEWHERE,
I JUST THROW UP.

I DIDN'T DO MY HOMEWORK BECAUSE

MY MOM WAS WATCHING TV.

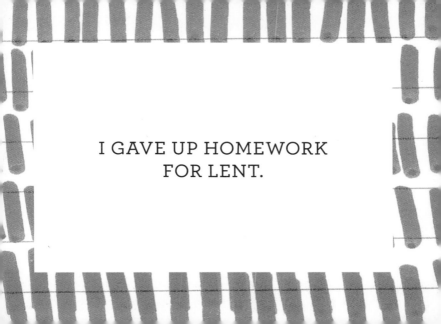

I GAVE UP HOMEWORK
FOR LENT.

I WANT A
CAN EAT MY

DOG SO HE
HOMEWORK.

I DID MY HOMEWORK
IN MY HEAD!

MY MOM ACCIDENTALLY
THREW OUT MY HOMEWORK.
SHE TOLD ME TO SAY
I NEVER GOT A PAPER.

I WAS ON THE LOSING TEAM,
SO I SWITCHED TEAMS.

I'M NOT CRYING.
I'M JUST MAKING NOISES.

I DON'T NEED TOWELS—
MY DOG TAUGHT
ME THE SHAKE.

MY TEST IS WRINKLED

BECAUSE I GAVE IT A HUG.

GROWING UP

WANTS, WISHES, AND WINS

I SCORED THREE GIRLS
AT SOCCER TODAY!

MY DREAM IS TO HELP PEOPLE
MAKE THEIR BEDS.

WHEN I GROW UP, I'M ONLY GOING TO
EAT SPICY FOOD AND USE
PERMANENT MARKERS.

ONE DAY,

I'LL BE AN ICE CREAM SCOOPER.

I WANT TO BE A TEACHER,
BUT MY FIRST NAME
ISN'T "MRS."

I NEED A MINIVAN

SO I CAN DRIVE ALL MY FRIENDS MYSELF.

I WANT TO BE A FARMER,
BUT I HATE VEGETABLES!

ALL THE TEETH IN MY MOUTH
ARE NOW ADULTS.

I CAN'T WAIT TO BE A DAD
SO I CAN PICK THE RESTAURANTS.

I'M OLDER NOW.
I WATCH NETFLIX.

OF COURSE I'M NOT A GROWN-UP!
DO YOU SEE A MUSTACHE?

WHEN THESE ROCKS
TURN INTO DIAMONDS,
I'LL BE RICH.

IF I DON'T GO TO SLEEP,
I WON'T GET OLD.

THIS IS THE
OLDEST AND SMARTEST
I'VE EVER BEEN.

LOVE

WHEN YOUR HEART FEELS ON FIRE

I'D MARRY MY DOG,
BUT I DON'T WANT TO
KISS HIM LIKE THAT.

WHEN YOU LOVE SOMEONE,
YOU MARRY THEM SO YOU DON'T
HAVE TO GIVE THEM BACK
TO THEIR PARENTS.

MARRIAGE MEANS

YOU ALWAYS HAVE SOMEONE
TO PLAY SOCCER WITH.

IT'S EASY TO GET MARRIED.
JUST ASK!

I'M GOING ONLINE TO SEE
IF KIDS GET MARRIED
WHEN THEY'RE SIX.

I CAN'T MARRY HIM.

HE CRIES TOO MUCH.

NO ONE WANTS TO DEAL WITH THAT!

YOU CAN KISS ME.

I'M USED TO IT!

I'M FEELING A NEW FEELING AND
I DON'T KNOW WHAT IT IS.

HE KISSED MY HAND
AND NOW I NEED HANITIZER!

I'LL MARRY
I DON'T

A PENGUIN,
CARE.

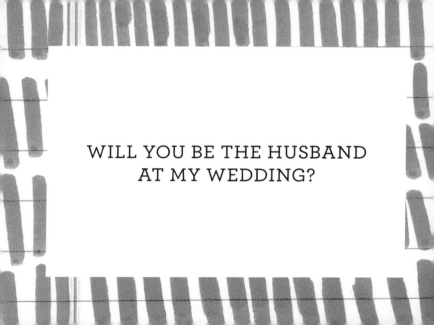

WILL YOU BE THE HUSBAND
AT MY WEDDING?

MY DOG LOVES ME SO MUCH

THAT HE SHARES HIS WATER
BOWL WITH ME.

MY PARENTS DO THEIR
KISSING IN THE KITCHEN.

I KNOW WHAT A COUGAR IS—
AND NOT THE ANIMAL.

WHAT DO YOU DO WHEN YOU'RE DATING?
JUST RIDE AROUND
IN CARS TOGETHER?

YOU HAVE TO GET SHOT
WITH AN ARROW
BEFORE YOU CAN FALL IN LOVE.

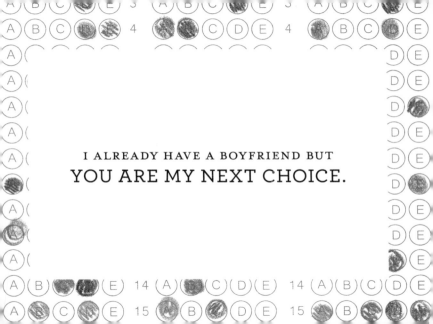

I ALREADY HAVE A BOYFRIEND BUT
YOU ARE MY NEXT CHOICE.

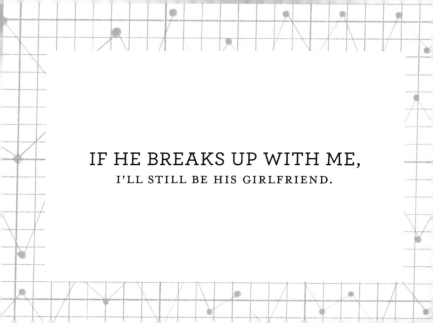

IF HE BREAKS UP WITH ME,

I'LL STILL BE HIS GIRLFRIEND.

I DON'T WANT A HUSBAND—
I WANT HELP
AROUND THE HOUSE.

PEOPLE HOLD HANDS SO
THEIR RINGS DON'T FALL OFF.

LOVE IS WHEN

YOU LOVE SOMEONE
EVEN WHEN YOU'RE TIRED.

MYSTERIES

THINGS TO THINK ABOUT WHILE
THE TEACHER IS TALKING

WHY CAN'T WE HAVE THE SOCIAL
AND NOT THE STUDIES?

DO ALL BOOKS END
WITH "THE END"?

WHY ARE WISHES

MADE OF PENNIES?

DO ADULTS HAVE
PLAY DATES?

HOW WILL I MAKE NEW FRIENDS
IF I CAN'T TALK TO
STRANGERS?

DO HORSEFLIES LOOK LIKE
TINY HORSES?

HOW DID A FROG GET
ALL THE WAY IN MY THROAT?

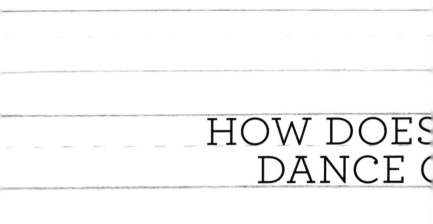

HOW DOES
DANCE C

THE PEE-PEE

AGAIN?

IF I'M OUT OF BREATH,

WHY DO I HAVE MORE?

WHY DON'T I SEE BIRDS

WHEN I BUMP MY HEAD?

DOES SANTA KNOW
WE MOVED?

HOW DOES THE TOOTH FAIRY GET IN
IF THE WINDOW IS CLOSED?

SOMETIMES I DON'T KNOW
IF I'M LAUGHING OR COUGHING.

I HOPE I DON'T
CRY TO DEATH.

WHY DON'T WE CELEBRATE
AMERICA'S HALF BIRTHDAY?

WHAT DID PEOPLE EAT IN THE NINETIES?

WHY DOES MY JAW KEEP
DROPPING WHEN I'M TIRED?

WHEN WILL I GET
MY ADULT BONES?

DOES THE BABY EVER FALL OUT

WHEN SHE'S WALKING AROUND?

MY FINGER IS GETTING
MORE AND MORE PUFFY . . .
IS IT PREGNANT?

SIGN LANGUAGE IS
CURSIVE, RIGHT?

SHE SAID IT WAS A PIECE OF CAKE.
BUT THERE WAS
NO CAKE AT ALL.

WILL THE TOOTH I SWALLOWED
SLICE UP MY WHOLE BODY?

HOW WILL I
REMEMBER EVERYTHING

IN JUST ONE BRAIN?

CELEBRATIONS

THE DAYS WHEN
THE RULES DON'T APPLY

I'M CHANGING MY BIRTHDAY THIS YEAR.
WAITING SUCKS.

ON MY BIRTHDAY,
I AM THE DECISION MAKER.

FOR MY BIRTHDAY,
I WANT AN APPLE JUICE RELAX PARTY.

I GET ALL THE ICING.
IT'S MY CAKE!

THIS IS THE DAY
MY MOM BECAME A MOM!

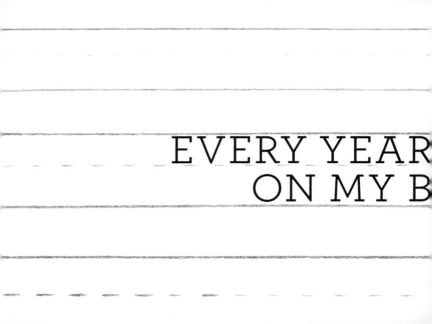

EVERY YEAR
ON MY B

THROW UP
RTHDAY.

IF I DON'T BLOW OUT THE CANDLES,
WILL THE CAKE
CATCH ON FIRE?

IT SMELLS LIKE
HAPPY BIRTHDAY IN HERE!

MY BIRTHDAY
IS IN THREE SLEEPS!

CAN I SKIP A BIRTHDAY

IF MY MOM SAYS IT'S OKAY?

THE RESTAURANT WAS SO FANCY,

IT HAD AUTOMATIC SOAP.

SUMMER IS JUST
MORE SLEEP AND
MORE ICE CREAM.

I'M WEARING MY
SUNGLASSES ALL DAY
BECAUSE IT'S STILL SUMMER
UNTIL SEPTEMBER.

THE SUN ALWAYS FOLLOWS ME
EVEN WHEN I ZIGZAG!

THERE IS NO SCHOOL
THE DAY AFTER THANKSGIVING
SO EVERYONE CAN POOP.

SANTA IS REAL, BUT

HIS FLYING SLED IS STUPID.

YOU ARE
NOT THE BOSS OF ME,

SANTA IS.

ELVES ARE LIKE,

I LOVE MY JOB!

YOU'RE LUCKY—YOU GET TO CELEBRATE
CHRISTMAS AND HARMONICA.

THAT'S WHAT I LOVE ABOUT CHRISTMAS—
THE PRESENTS COME
AUTOMAGICALLY!

BESTIE

THE ONE WHO WILL TALK TO YOU
WHILE YOU'RE IN TIME-OUT

WE ARE BEST FRIENDS—
WE EVEN PEE TOGETHER!

WE SHARE EVERYTHING,
EXCEPT FOR TISSUES.

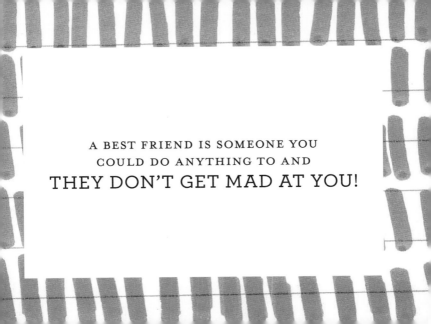

A BEST FRIEND IS SOMEONE YOU
COULD DO ANYTHING TO AND
THEY DON'T GET MAD AT YOU!

MY BEST FRIEND'S NAME IS MATT—
I THINK.

BEST FRIENDS ARE
LIKE MARSHMALLOWS

IN YOUR LUCKY CHARMS.

HOW MANY FRIENDS
AM I ALLOWED TO HAVE?

WE ARE BFFAEAEDS

(BEST FRIENDS FOREVER AND EVER—
AND EVEN DURING SUMMER).

IF YOU TELL
I'LL ZIP IT
AND SHOOT IT

ME A SECRET,
LOCK IT,
N A ROCKET!

I ASKED MY PARENTS IF WE COULD
HAVE HIM IN OUR FAMILY.

LET'S HAVE A SLEEPOVER,
DINNER-OVER,
PLAY-OVER!

AT SCHOOL
I TALK ABOUT MATH.
ON PLAY DATES
I TALK ABOUT BATMAN.

LET'S PLAY POOL PARTY.
I'LL BE THE LIFEGUARD AND
YOU BE THE POOL.

FAMILY

THE PEOPLE WHO NEVER FORGET
YOUR BIRTHDAY

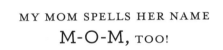

MY MOM SPELLS HER NAME
M-O-M, TOO!

I HAD A GIRLS' DAY WITH MY MOM
AND ATE A LOT OF CHEESE.

I LOVE MY DAD BECAUSE

HE TAUGHT ME HOW TO PEE.

MY DAD HAS KNOWN ME
SINCE I WAS ZERO.

MY DAD IS SO STRONG,

HE CAN EVEN PICK UP TEACHERS.

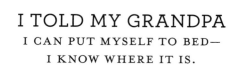

I TOLD MY GRANDPA
I CAN PUT MYSELF TO BED—
I KNOW WHERE IT IS.

I WISH I COULD BRING
MY PARENTS TO A LIBRARY AND
CHECK OUT NEW ONES.

THE GRAMMY AWARDS ARE FOR THE
VERY BEST GRANDMA.

I HAVE TWO GRANDMAS:
ONE WHO PICKS ME UP
AND ONE WHO HAS A MUSTACHE.

WHEN MY GRANDMA DIES,
I DON'T WANT HER TO
REST IN PEAS.

I THOUGHT OLD PEOPLE WERE SUPPOSED
TO BE NICE AND FRIENDLY.
WHAT HAPPENED TO
MY GRANDMA?

I PROMISED MOM THAT KARATE
IS ONLY FOR HURTING ROBBERS—
NOT MY BROTHER.

MY BROTHER
WAS BORN NAKED.

I CAN'T B
MOM SWALLO

IEVE MY
WED A BABY.

THIS THANKSGIVING
I'M THANKFUL FOR MY BROTHER . . .
MAYBE MY SISTER NEXT YEAR.

I LOVE MY SISTER,

BUT SHE HAS A SMALL BRAIN.

I'M THE RING BEAR THIS WEEKEND!
ROAR!

I HOPE MY PARENTS BRING ME

SOMEWHERE COOL

ON SATURDAY,

LIKE AFRICA.

FEELINGS

THE UPS AND DOWNS OF THE DAY

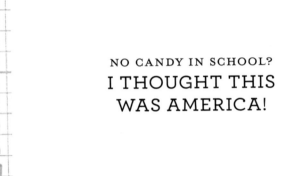

NO CANDY IN SCHOOL?
I THOUGHT THIS
WAS AMERICA!

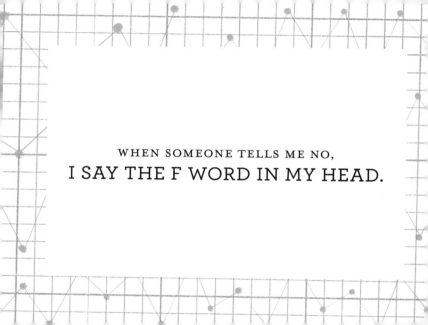

WHEN SOMEONE TELLS ME NO,
I SAY THE F WORD IN MY HEAD.

I HAVE A SECRET DANCE
FOR MY BAD DAYS—
IT HELPS.

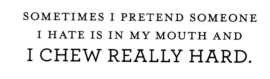

SOMETIMES I PRETEND SOMEONE
I HATE IS IN MY MOUTH AND
I CHEW REALLY HARD.

WHEN I'M MAD,
I JUST TAKE A REALLY LONG NAP.

I WISH I HAD
MORE MIDDLE FINGERS!

SHE FIGHTS WITH ME

LIKE IT'S IN HER SCHEDULE!

I HURT MY OWN FEELINGS.

I DON'T LIKE BEING FIVE.

TOO MUCH MATH TO DO.

I WISH I WAS
A PENCIL SHARPENER.
THEY NEVER GET TIRED.

I DON'T KNOW WHAT I SAID.
I WASN'T LISTENING
TO MYSELF.

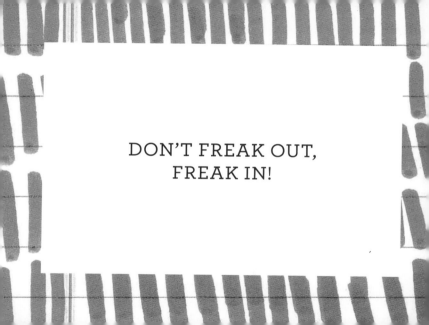

DON'T FREAK OUT,
FREAK IN!

I NEED A BREAK.

MY BRAIN IS SHAKING.

TEACHERS ALWAYS
COME INTO MY DAY AND
MAKE IT BORING.

I HAVE AN
OUCH ON MY HEART.

I PUT MYSELF IN
SOMEONE ELSE'S SHOES
AND THEY DIDN'T FIT.

I DON'T LIKE HUGS FROM
REALLY TALL PEOPLE.

THE HOKEY POKEY

CALMS ME DOWN.

I CRIED SO MUCH

MY WHOLE BODY IS WET.

WHEN I WANT TO BE IN A GOOD MOOD,
I JUST PICTURE A
GENIE IN A BIKINI.

CONCLUSIONS

DEEP THOUGHTS AND DISCOVERIES

GEORGE WASHINGTON LOOKS LIKE
A GRANDMA.

BATMAN AND SUPERMAN
HAVE THE SAME LAST NAME!

SIX MORE LEGS

AND I'LL BE A SPIDER.

I GOT IT!

TODAY WAS YESTERDAY'S TOMORROW.

PICTURE BOOKS?

THAT WAS SO LAST YEAR.

WE HAVE
LOTS OF TASTE BUDS—
ONE FOR EVERY SINGLE TASTE.

SNOWMEN DON'T
LIKE HOT COCOA.

SEAFOOD
MAKES ME SEASICK.

BANANAS WILL NEVER GET
SUNBURNED.

WIND MAKES ALL
THE PLANTS DANCE.

MILK IS COLD BECAUSE
COWS ARE NAKED.

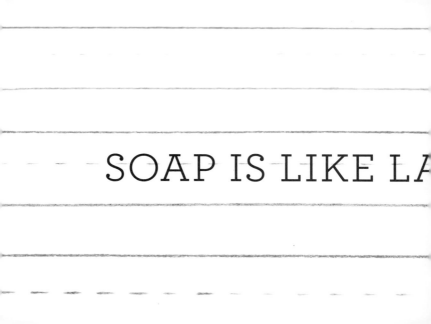

SOAP IS LIKE LA

A FOR GERMS.

RAISINS ARE JUST
ELDERLY GRAPES.

BIRTH HAPPENS WHEN A
BABY IS DONE COOKING.

MY BUTT HAS
A LINE OF SYMMETRY!

I LOST MY VOICE SATURDAY BUT
I FOUND IT IN MY ROOM.

MY HAIR IS SO LONG BECAUSE
I WATER IT IN THE SHOWER.

IF I WEAR MY
BIKINI TO SCHOOL,
I DON'T NEED AN UMBRELLA!

THE DINOSAURS
GOT EXTINCT
TO MAKE ROOM FOR US.

I LIVE IN A BRICK HOUSE

SO NO ONE
CAN BLOW IT DOWN.

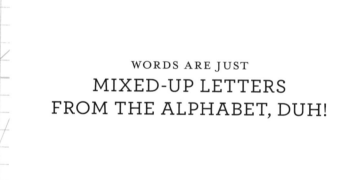

WORDS ARE JUST
MIXED-UP LETTERS
FROM THE ALPHABET, DUH!

READING IS
A SECRET LANGUAGE
THAT BABIES CAN'T KNOW.

SWINGS ARE SO FUN,
AND YOU JUST NEED TO SIT DOWN!

IF YOU TAKE ME TO A FANCY RESTAURANT,
I'LL JUST BURP
THE WHOLE TIME.

I DIDN'T GET A SHOT—
THAT WOULD BE DANGEROUS!
IT WAS JUST A NEEDLE.

KIDNEYS ARE
WASHING MACHINES
FOR OUR BODIES.

TO HAVE A GOOD DAY,
DO A MILLION GOOD THINGS.

ACKNOWLEDGMENTS

Thank you to all the teachers, parents, grandparents, babysitters, and siblings who have shared and submitted their favorite quotes through our @LiveFromSnackTime Instagram account. You've made us laugh endlessly.

Thank you to our own teachers and parents, who have supported *all* our accomplishments and still remind us that we were once just as guilty of saying hilarious and outlandish things.

Thank you to Judy Pueschel and her team at Stonesong for countless conversations, advice, and encouragement throughout the process. Thank you to everyone at Potter, including Angelin Borsics, Lise Sukhu, Danielle Deschenes, Cathy Hennessy, Kevin Garcia, Luisa Francavilla, and many more, for having the faith and sense of humor to create this book.

To my partner and friend, Greg, you have turned a teacher into an author. Thank you for transforming my messy observation notebook into a true gem.

An elementary school teacher in New York City, ALYSSA COWIT started the Instagram account @LiveFromSnackTime with GREG DUNBAR, a digital marketing manager with Walt Disney Studios. Cowit lives in Manhattan and Dunbar lives in Los Angeles.